Full Circle Undivided

Full Circle Undivided

Poems

VOLUME 1

Wendy E. Slater

Full Circle Undivided
Copyright © 2021 by Wendy E. Slater
traduka.com

All rights reserved. No part of this book may be reproduced in any form or by any means, electronic or mechanical, including photocopying, recording, or by any information storage and retrieval system, without permission in writing from the publisher.

Wendy E. Slater books are available for order through
Ingram Press Catalogues

Traduka Publishing
traduka@traduka.com

Paper ISBN: 978-1-943512-03-4
E-book: 978-1-943512-04-1

BOOK DESIGN BY STREETLIGHT GRAPHICS
AUTHOR PHOTO BY JEFF WOODWARD
COVER PHOTO BY WENDY E. SLATER

For the Truth
And
The Path
To it

CONTENTS

THE DOT 1

   1   Silence whitewashes against my soul 3

   2   A decaying carcass 5

   3   I, once, consumed with guilt 6

   4   The pain 8

THE ARC 9

   5   In the illness 11

   6   My body, my temple 12

   7   I am in the vortex 13

   8   And I read into my mind 15

   9   Strapped and buckled 16

  10 Thank you 18

  11 in the darkest hour 19

  12 The hawk 20

  13 In the moment 21

  14 I want to scream 22

THE TRAJECTORY 23

  15 I am in the cave 25

FULL CIRCLE 27

  16 Unnoticed 29

17	I dream of	30
18	I wonder about	31
19	I dream of sitting by lit embers	32
20	The whole thing feels	33
21	An exercise	34
22	Lift me up	35
23	It's gone now	36
24	If I could	37
25	Holding the sacred	38
26	Nakedly	39
27	I am soft	40
28	The beloved	41
29	I kick up my heels	42
30	A faucet's been turned on	43
31	You are right here	44
32	Am I going to get lost in you?	45
33	I am grounding again	47
34	It happened so suddenly	48
35	There is a part	50
36	I wake	51
37	Today I washed	52
38	In your room again	53
39	I am with God	54

40	It's been about	55
41	Do you read my notes	56
42	Walking out	58
43	I wake	59
44	There aren't words	60
45	I wish	61
46	Beyond that night	62
47	I am densing down	63
48	I am fat	64
49	With axe and pick	65
50	He is so fractured	67
51	I simply	68
52	Zero passion and clarity and light	69
53	Oh, God	71
54	I am small	72
55	The heart	73
56	It's whole again	74
57	It's happening again	75
58	Tonight reminds me	76
59	The moon is full	77
60	Longing	78
61	It's opaque	80
62	I walk the hall	81

63　I wish　82
64　Why aren't you　83
65　My bed　84
66　GRIEF　86
67　I am done　87
68　The full circle　89
69　The full circle scrawls　91
70　Arrogance aside　93
71　The truth　94
72　I need to shut down this joint, buster　96
73　It's like I am on the merry-go-round　98

THE DOT

THE DOT

1

Silence whitewashes against my soul
As the break of a wave
Slamming down against the sand.

When will all grow quiet and tamed
As the shade of a sunstroked journey through hell: a day?
Only after the last exit,
The final breathing in of this violating force
After the last and final breakdown
Of separate quakes, erupting into a tidal wave.

This eruption contains the capacity
To destroy, to ravage, to consume everything,
But a pen,
A sporadically-charged force of lightning,
The electrical igniting force of this exodus
Is to purge, seething and writhing, with repentance
The cold flat words.

Silenced harmonious waves fluttering
Through the lips, past the mind's horizon,
No man's land, territory of aborted thoughts.
Bloodless thoughtless acts convert to sweet hysteria.

The contradiction twists and bribes
With a tempestuous resonance of an impregnated wave
Gathering force and
Breaking down
At the edge,
Destroying only to rebuild.
Salted nectar nibbles at my soul, at the dunes:
My foundation for growth and will.
This feigned nectar will hoard all, absorb as a body, a unit, a single tsunami
Contained in four walls:
Mine, ours, theirs, his
Humid, moist, clammy, cold.

Four walls between me, my physical being, my thoughts, and my words.
Four layers between the cold and hot, the rational and raw.

A stilting shift
In the stillborn motion of the air
I breathe
On the shoreline, a tangled web of hair
Catches words, shades the misconception of ideas, miscarriage of
Dreams.

I sit crested and welded between
A deep breath and a shallow sigh,
A contemplation that traces
An outline of consciousness,
Like the suction, the shadow of a steel plate arched against the
Trespassing force of my lungs.
Words, letters, breaths seduced by a tongue
Collecting thoughts as a child gathering shells
Along the decaying shoreline.

She grasps onto the carapace
Clutching remnants of the emancipated act of 1983, the exodus,
As nothing to everything
Like my body to blankets
Waves to sand
Words to a tongue:
A net with baited line.

4:00 a.m. and the tide shifts
5:00 a.m. ripping slowly to a climax.

2

A decaying carcass
Shedding its guise
Feel
Sense
That rotting insecurity:
An unlatched door—
Stalking for prey: me.
You even cheat and deceive
The silhouettes of the disarrayed night.

Within the shadows
Thrives an internal warmth
Rooted deep
A flower blooms
Evoking both
Harmony and pain
Polarities in existence.

This too will wilt
Like the crest of a dawn
Molding into the morning dew,
Nature's emblem of birth
Uprising, rebelling against all that is manmade:
That which has raped you, your thoughts, your breath.

3

I, once, consumed with guilt,
Confessed it was me
Who sculpted the waves
Of innate desire which drove
Our lips to explode
With that counterfeit passion for love.

In retrospect:
The explosion
Thus, the contemplation,
A confrontation—
An excuse for you
Alone
To rise
Into a musing stance, a retching glance
As if you had caressed the match
Which torched the blaze
Of a brushfire in a heated chase.
I was your alibi, the accomplice,
And I extinguished it.

A frigid embrace with the bare facts:
A dyslexic jointing with your
Raw, hemorrhaging words,
Epileptic redundancies with each spasmodic utterance—
I rhythmically choked with
Your each and every convulsion
Down my throat.
And I was the one who
Confessed?

I see it now
Simply
As a reaffirmed echo
Of past,
And for future,
You have secured my suspicions.

I am not mute,
The absence of words
Is not devoid of thought—
This is an iron silence.
The penetration,
Cajoling dusty blue cataracts,
Is what cracked me.

RECALL? Do you admit
For once
Without demanding an entrance fee?
Or do you ever want to know
This refractory spirit
Which fed the fire by which you breathed,
The inner resources: yellow, white and burnished gold
Which I urgently and admittingly fished out
With the weight of a 20 lb. bass on a 19 lb.
Line
Tangled and caught
In the bloating and wrecked debris
Dividing us.
Cliché? Then in my mind so are you.

Floundering at its death, life breathed;
But I gasped in a starched net of your structured insanity,
Until I bleached up your harm, vomited up the memories
And salvaged the fire in the ashes which still smolders in my breast.

4

The pain,
It seems
Unbearable, impenetrable:
A knot entwined in my ass.
A searing weight
Rusted iron,
Branding hands,
On my rump.
Rearing
Towards the sky,
Stamping hooves,
Branded emblems,
Me, rounded up as cattle.

In a mirror
It is as if I can see behind their backs,
Tying knots, lassos, lariats
And the noose.
Ready at any moment
For herding, harvesting—even milking.
Cowboys loving
Their cowgirls.

According to those branding hands
I was grazing, simply whiling
Away from
Prime
Tender meat to be.
A fated hanging, I was told,
For any branded rump.

Never spoke of
Cows in India:
A land where those who are primed for the kill,
The dinner plate in the West,
Graze freely on city streets
However undernourished they may be.

THE ARC

5

In the illness,
  I am in my body
    Prone on the couch
      I must remember
          Recall
      I am the same woman
        Who planted asparagus
         Digging deep into the earth
           Sweaty and barebacked
             With blistered hands.

I scan my body for markers of the past:
     Blisters, calluses
   Scars are not reabsorbed

Now I measure time.

6

My body, my temple
Womanly worship
This beautiful body
Is not mine
Alone
You isolate me.
A virus, a toxin
Controls and batters me.
I am the Battered Woman
Constantly threatened
Full of your lies and excuses
And such demands.
You beat me up when I see people—
Fearing I will stray?
No bruises, bones whole,
"You seem fine," they think.
My heart is broken, heavy
With the weight of your needs.
Your lie is out.
I tell them, "No.
I will not get away.
I cannot run."
You have the things I love: me and us,
My body, my temple.
But one night,
I will push you out, lock you out.
I will be strong enough
To stand alone
And love and trust.

7

I am in the vortex
The hollow hidden entrance
To the black hole:
You.

I am not hungry
Food fills the kitchen
Not me.

I have not felt pain for
Years and months
Before I noticed
This demand for acknowledgment.

Unaware
Wrapped tight
With the woolen blanket,
The one your family knitted
To me, for me
One all too hot
Languid day
On this chilly night
It seems to go deeper
Pulled tight
I am invisible,
Robbed of my warmth
My flame
My fire
In the darkest, most private
Crevices of my body
The part I chose and choose
To share only with you.
In the darkest hour
Of the darkest space
You gave me away.

You are still my hero
Truly not the Don Juan on the white horse
Always the net
To catch me
Reluctantly, I suppose.

8

And I read into my mind
like an excerpt from a dense, thick novel
where one has to read the lines twice
to get past the confusion.

Us in my kitchen,
after watching her play
with my children,
the imaginary ones.

Asking
straight out like an arrow,
why weren't you ever that way with me?
thinking tender, loving, forgiving,
mine.

Honestly, she would open up to me,
like the east sun filling the bedroom in the morning:
bright, cheerful, welcome,
once I get past the shock.

Had I known all this before,
I would have created these same children
at eight. I would have been mother
by right rather than wrong.

9

Strapped and buckled in little red sandals with room to grow,
My small pink feet danced
Along and within
That white picket fence,
The grass was parched and poked
Into the tender
Pink toes.
In a big shingled house by the sea,
A house was large and we were so small
That your mother missed
While the jelly set and the table was stacked
And cleared.

The small pink lips
Parted from her small body.
I was always so tiny they hoped I would disappear
Naked and forever probably cold
Pressed against those tiles upstairs in August or July
On that summer island.
For once, I am in the bathroom without
Old salt baked against skin,
As I desperately draw myself closer to the source
Of clean water.
I was golden all over and over.

You were bruised and overripe
Like the fallen
Speckled fruits,
Flecked and pocked
That led and littered
The way to your summer home
Beach plum jam charring as her voice reached up and into and around
The leftovers.

Sharing family secrets with me while your mother washes up
My back to the wall, I barely reach the sink.
Big loud shoes climb up
The stairs and all over my bony golden shoulders

Your mother's hands are full of flour
She has beaten and mixed for hours
Dusted white hair, white skin
My little flat feet match the tub as I take
The blame for your family recipes,
Your mother's book.

I think you wanted to play with me.
The one and only day I came
With 6-year-old hopes of dolls, jacks, cookies and milk
I am under the watchful eye of your mother
With her too-tight and too-short gingham apron she wears as a big badge
And her dirty, pastry hands smeared all over me.
She spent so much time in the kitchen
Baking, basting, and frying
Her head in the oven checking the roast,
Perfectly timed, she misses.

In your room, you are locked.
Dressed again
I am dusted and displayed
Draped in a chair too big for the small and
Alone and swinging madly
My feet are in unison each time the door opens
On the way to the kitchen
With a brother, a sister, her mother's hands
Again
Filled with scents of leftover lunch
And dinner to be.

I chew my finger till it bleeds.
At 6,
I know I will disappear
With your secret family recipes,
Dinners I never had.
Family recipes just now digested
Of a meal I had forgotten
That I almost shared.

10

Thank you
Your words
  In passing
 Uplift my spirit.

11

in the darkest hour,
  when all is still,
and the night no longer
  lingers, but settles in,
the dawn springs forth
  like the jaguar
    unseen, stalking
 in the brush
    with the unknown.

12

The hawk
Soars above and into
  The beyond.
On its wings,
   I rest.
In its talons,
   I am safe and
     Protected.

13

In the moment
   Before
The arc
 Of the belonging
    The welcoming
 The dawning
   As the crest
  Of the newborn's
    Head
 Peaking.

14

I want to scream
  I want to howl
    Like a dog
  Chained to a stump
      Of a man.

THE TRAJECTORY

15

I am in the cave
Walled and barred
Weathered and worn
Cold
Dampened by the time
You pressed your
Stiff corpse-like body up into the mine.
Was I eight or nine?

Does age matter?
Now I am 37
And I search and feel the walls of this cave,
The texture reveals my history.
There are no words, no textbooks, no glossy photographs
To explain why
There is no memory
There is no light.

I have arrived at this moment
Like a spelunker
Floodlight strapped to my head,
Chains and ropes
Link me to the present
As a descendent
Into the undiscovered.

Others have trespassed
Old graffiti and scars
Serve as signposts.
I do not get lost,
Markers that misguided me along the way:
Beer cans, vomit, and a punching bag,
Scotch bottles, empty and abandoned,
A television still playing the national anthem.
Shame, shame, shame.
This is old and too well-preserved.

In the rage and anger,
The deep vein,
I was unable to approach this cave,
My womb, my breasts, my sensuality,
To know this woman inside
And out.

Hours pass and these 37-year-old hands
And this 37-year-old smile
Scrub and sing
And mingle the salty tears of a woman with that of the child.
Seeing for the first time, this beauty
That is me, that is not a mine
To be excavated and harnessed
And abandoned and neglected.
It is me, it is mine
Alone
A sacredness.

With the rope linked to the present,
I attach the rags that have cleaned off
The graffiti, the slander:
A shame, the shame
Hoisted up
Like a proud sail
In a deep gust.
Sighs heave from me.
I am beautiful and tender and loving and loved by me.

I am whole and clean
And womanly.
My history is known
Like braille
Codings
That release me from a darkness.
A place that lacked the vocabulary to explain.

FULL CIRCLE

16

Unnoticed
My feet walked the perimeter
Of the garden
While you weeded
The unwanted.
Already you had tilled the earth,
Ready for a new planting,
The new planting
As my hands reached deep into
The soil and united
With earth, heaven, stars, sky,
And you.
Forgiveness.

17

I dream of
Coves,
Farms and naked babies,
Draped over my arm
And in the cradle of your shoulder
Feet planted into a soil
Deeply tilled and touched
By your hands and history.

A swirling groan from deep
Within as I see
Your eyes and feel your soul,
A tenderness and truth
Naked to the bone

    Lip planted to lip
      Love sings.

18

I wonder about
Claustrophobia and commitment,
Well-like depths.

I dream of quarter moons
Rising up over
The mound
Shooting stars and ginger tea,
Us being embraced between
And amongst
Sky and dirt.

The forgotten, but known,
      The untouched
      The sacred
      The holy union
      Of heaven and earth
      Within and without you.

19

I dream of sitting by lit embers
Knitting sweaters
Out of yarns and loving you.

Your fire is in me now
Blazing and vibrant
Clear and still
Joyous.

I think of estuaries,
Grey hair, grandchildren,
Rocking chairs,
Stone houses
And hearts.

Are we together again?

20

The whole thing feels
   Like a sacred marriage:
       A ceremony and celebration of wholeness.
 It was only after the forgiving
 Of self and burial of self
 Judgment and judgment
      Of others
   That I was fully able to enter
   This sacred grounding
And your arms to accept
A wholeness within and
    To accept that within
      Others. To unite straight-
      Forwardly rather than
      Fracturedly from an angle,
      To surrender to the heart and
      Breathe with the belly. A rhythm
      Begins, undulating
         Waves, strong and consistent
           Buoyant and full.

21

An exercise
To stay
    In the moment
  For being in the heart
    Of the heart
    And with the breath.

22

Lift me up
Like you did once before
In your arms
Cradled and rocked
Into that
Soft womanly
Place:
A tenderness, my tenderness,
A celebrated cause and effect—
Fruition of forgiveness.

23

It's gone now—
A memory,
I wish I'd caught it
On film, a snapshot,
A slide to project, a positive
To process
Again and again.

In that moment, where time is not,
We are eternal
Forever embraced,
A blessed union.

It is when I step out and
Beyond my heart
To the mind that
I attach and yearn and crave and lust
For an object
That is at home with me and
In me.

It is like I am looking
From behind
Through but not beyond
A two-way mirror,
Separated, observant, apart, and hidden
By obscurations of
The ego.

From the heart,
I know we would
Go deeper
If we could.

24

If I could
I would strap my oxygen
Tank to my back, mask to
My front and clasp my
Hand to yours and
Descend together into
These wild depths of
The unknown to
Remember, to dance
Wildly and swim
Through passages
And wrecks and
Scars and
Spin and swirl
Into the light's
Splattered rays.
I would trust you
To be
My guide and companion
And to make your home
In this sacred place.

25

Holding the sacred
Like a scepter,

I wonder
and
Dance
and
Blaze
and
Sigh
and
Glow

All the while.

26

Nakedly
  Exposed and covered
    By a loose sheet
In bed
    As my body hums
And dances
    With your memory:
    A signature now
      In my vibration.

My breasts
     Ripe and round
  Longing for your hands
To cup and stroke
    Your tongue
To lick and lap.

To have
This aching
Tenderly released.

I am soft
    Sensual
  I am grounded
  I am a rock
    Solid
    Woman
Screaming through time
    And space
Orbiting and rocketing
   On a trajectory
   Out of gravity
Propelled and powered
  By your touch.

28

The beloved
Is orange like monk's robes
In the center
Redroot red
On the outer petals
Flowered,
Ten-fingered
Dirt from the garden
Under the nails.

Strong muscled
Tawny lean
And soft fuzzed
Legs strapped and
Wrapped
Along my body:
Our world.

29

I kick up my heels
It's confirmed
I am stamped
W.E.S. approval.

I am
 A
Womanly woman.

Sacred, Earthy
Salty
Complete
With or without
You.

30

A faucet's been turned on
 Orange erupts from the spigot,
Once inert words and phrases
         Walled to the womb
           The cavity for over a decade
 Now dance in the flames,
  The light has softened
           The angles.
 There is no severity.
  It is not dark.

The locale is there
And everywhere.
It is rooted and soaring in
Me and us,
And all
The cosmos.

I want your baby
Seeded and blooming
In this sacred home,
In a place of
Honor.

31

You are right here
In these words
And phrases
Even the period
Flowing from my womb
And in my heart.

Pages flip as I trace
Our history, really our moment.
Words dance and hum
And recreate
As I come
Into a balance.

32

Am I going to get lost in you?
          Or on You?
    I have a compass,
      North Star.
This Way
     Is mapless terrain.
That Way
The topography is evident.
I will need crampons to scale the hardened
Territories.

I ache,
My life purpose is larger than us,
Larger than getting lost to you
In
Coves, farms, and babies
And your arms which bring me to my
Knees in sweet surrender.
Is this another lesson,
In selflessness,
Relinquishing of the ego?
A giving up
Of those
I cherish—
And yet, I am wildly
Connected and present.

In this other place called my heart
Our work is not done.
You have the key
To the unification,
To the beloved
True self.

And I hold the
Balm, your balm, to ease

Out the visions
And attachments to past
Criticism, severity, and ivory
Towers of imprisonment.

I want to free you
Because
I love you.

I want you to be whole
And vibrant
And settled into
Your core.

I want to be that wild
Fiery woman to
Thaw
You, your heart.
For now. Just for now.
And always.

33

I am grounding again
    North is North
    South is South
As I water my garden
You stretch me to
The heavens and beyond
In your eternal embrace.

34

It happened so suddenly
  Like a heavy fire door
      Slamming shut.

So unpredictably
Like
Catching a fleeting glimpse
Of a shooting star
Arcing over the sky.
Traceless.

I am in love
L-O-V-E
You are in the closet,
Dark and hiding
In retreat
But your glow,
The light gives you away.

I see you across the ocean
Scrawling across the sky
You are each and every
Star
Glimmering with potential.

This stone door
On your heart
Calls for thawing,
My tender touch.
Fingers
Want to
Dance and crawl
Across your chest
To heal, to soothe,
To celebrate.

Instead,
I am on my back
Touching
The heavens
And counting stars
With the fleeting
Wave of my hand.
Palm against sky
My heart is with yours.

35

There is a part,
A fraction
Of me
That thinks I could have
Stayed forever
And gotten lost
To the green and lapis sea,
Coming in and out,
The ancient rocks,
The deep wells
Into your eyes.

There is a part of me
That is there with you.
Living and loving
Day in and out.

36

I wake
Assuming I have been battered and beaten
  From the invasion.
Dinner for 10,
Strung out arms and legs
Girlish, small, supple, round, and of course, the womanly,
On stools, chairs,
  Nothing matches, but the food,
      Little of it.
  To the 9,
    I am misunderstood
But accepted as one of the gaggle of joints and appendages.
We know I speak a different language,
    I hail from a different galaxy
One they want
    To own or ridicule
        And diminish.
For starters, they want a passport, an entry.
They do not understand
    It is in the heart.

37

Today I washed
The skirt
You slid off
And onto me.

It was mingled
With salt and sweat
And our ecstasy.

I was reluctant
So
This morning I buried
My nose
And smothered
Deep into the scents
And softness and you
And us all over again.

I ache for you
To feel your fingers
Ride up and under
Stretching and mingling.

38

In your room again
It's dark
With a glow of orange
Everywhere
We are at the center
The heart
Pulsing and beating
Blood and ecstatic
Air
Through the veins
And lungs
And core.
It's me and you.
Nothing more
Nothing less.
Nothing and everything.

39

I am with God
Now
You have seeded me
And rekindled
The knowing,
It swims and oozes
Into all those
Hidden places
Revealing pain and glory
Ready to embrace,
When I truly
And fully
Surrender
To the knowing
It's of me
Always
And never apart.

40

It's been about
10 days
28 poems definitely
Since we embraced
The beloved.

Today if your hands
Were near,
If I looked into you
Would I surrender
Again and again
And again?

I want to be near
To explain
I'm losing my mind
To my heart.

41

Do you read my notes
And letters
Again
And
Again
For clues and indications?

Do you bundle up
And stretch out on the mound
At night
In the quiet with the moon
Counting stars
Shooting and still
Recounting words and gazes
And touches?
Again and again and again?

Do you climb up
Into bed
And come
To me
Longing
For that still vibrant
Place within us
And me
In your eyes?
Again and again and again and again?

Do you know
How I ache for
You tenderly
And longingly?
Again and again and again and again and again?

I want to see
You
And be
In you
Always and all ways.

42

Walking out
Into the garden
I think of you
With each step

Running up to the water
I am with you
With each stride

And into the woods
You have me
As
I dance
Wildly and
So slowly.

43

I wake
In the night
To a full moon rising
Up.
The fields have been hayed.
Time has stopped.
I am on the mound
Again
As quarter moons rise and arc
Stars dance
And
We mingle
And murmur.

44

There aren't words
To carry that
Magnitude
Of grief and loss
Into the heart of the matter.

Ivory towers tumble to the grounds
Caving under
The impact
Of untold calculations.

Voices holler, wail, and scream
Lovers embrace.
There is such a loss
Of reason,
Of my voice.

45

I wish
That I could ignore this
Sweep it
Swiftly and concisely
Under the corner of a rug,
The oriental in the kitchen,
Hidden, tidy
Pretense

Or

Be
The maidenhead
At the bow of the ship
Arcing effortlessly
Through and above the
Waves
Steady, focused
Wooden.

We are still counting the dead
In our minds, on our fingers,
And in our families.
The nation of my heart is unified
With dignified compassion
And grief
For each and every one.

46

Beyond that night
  Of quarter moons
You have given
  Nothing
To indicate
A maturity
Like the ancient
Redwood, wise and solid,
To wrap myself around.
There is no scent to follow,
No clue to unfold,
No soft shelter to shield me,
No roots to ground me.
I am still
With myself.

47

I am densing down
    Feeling separate
        And apart.

Last night a plane
    Streamed across
        The sky
   And I counted stars
One for the night together
Two for the bodies entwined
Three for the union
Four for eternity
Five for joy
    And the list goes on
    Into the infinite.

48

I am fat
        Again
Ugly
Unintelligible
  Inarticulate
Bound and gagged by
    Limitations—
Not self-imposed,
A compromise of survival.

I question motives
 And my sanity.
"All's in order," he says.
Just as it should be.

Am I too
   Fragile and beaten
 Down for you
   To embrace?
That's the point.
So, I stay in my position,
   Tethered and tied.

But if you were
  Here
Even for an instant
  I would rise
Like the phoenix
   From the ashes
Not because of you,
But because of
   Me.

49

With axe and pick,
Shovel, too,
I venture into the dark realm.
There is no fear.
It is inert, a vestige
A memory surfaced within.

I dig with intention
Move years of anger, frozen now,
That has concealed
The truth.

This pumiced anger, a dark polished center on my heart,
Liberates the hidden,
What is revealed is simple and
Confused, a blur; in one way I get a glimpse,
A hint like the Loch Ness Monster rising up—
Was it an illusion, a doctored photo, or
The truth?

A patheticness that I see in another's mother, sister, family:
An utter sham.
It is so clear, the fury
Is theirs—
A patheticness of a wannabe.

This is where my psychicness betrayed me.
I doubt now
That others have been able to see
What I see in her, them.

The once gashed and gaping wound
Surfaces with a strained knowing
That I will no longer protect them
At my expense
Of health, intelligence, being.

To copy me, to wannabe me,
They have to find their hearts.

50

He is so fractured
    Splattered and wrecked
  That he litters
   Himself
  Up and down
   The road
  Again and again.
He is the great divide
   Between us and within
    Him.
His heart is like the grandest
   Of canyons
   In a drought
    In summer—
Empty and so
Parched.

I simply
Want
To be
Naked with you
Again
Unencumbered and honest
Stillness lying in and amongst
    Stillness
Like long stalks of grass,
Swaying in the wind,
Under the moon,
In the sun, stalks stripped back and exposed
Under the clouds and in the rain
Planted and seeding
Side-by-side in unison.

52

Zero passion and clarity and light
      Like the night—
But truthful in your distance.

No hint
Now there is no indication
No cosmic imprint
No trace
No tangible history
      Of us.

But you did whisper
Sweet nothings
      Zero gravity in a timeless place,
Soaring and vibrant and yawning and unioned.
But, in this earthly grounded place
Salt, sweat, and tears yearn
To mingle in an earthy way:
Sensual, revealed, open, vulnerable,
Breathing one exhale
At a time.

The valise of my heart:
      This trunk of undying longing
        For reciprocal union
        With the beloved
   Is unpacked and neatly folded back into
      Closed drawers in closed chambers.
The plane ticket exchanged
  A credit to my accounting.

I am on the couch
With The Pooch
Thinking not with my heart, but with the mind,
Is this all life is?
Aborted treks
      A tourist visa into the terrain of the beloved
      A tease

I want to be naturalized like a trueborn citizen:
Any offspring of the beloved.

I want to sing and dance
      And arc and sway
           Like a long swing from an old maple tree
           Able to explore freely
           The depths and ranges
           Of the starry night and cosmos
           With you as my witness and
           Myself.

I know now the beloved simply is
Radiant and full in me,
Waiting to sing and scream
Through the imagined ages and depths
Of stillness.
Thank you
For the invitation
To see myself.

Oh, God
To be in your arms
Rocking and swaying
Arcing towards each imagined
Infinite yawn of the galaxy
Darkness as black as any night,
Brilliant white lights,
Me with legs bent back
Gripping two long thick ropes
That hold the seat
Of the swing: momentum.

I have gathering force to propel me forward
Simply by imagining
You and where the touch will allow
Me to be.
In the flesh, because we are of the earth, too,
My sense of adventure and anticipation
Prepares me
               Heart to heart
               Feet to feet
               Hand to eye
               Yoked and loving
         As we stretch and yawn
                   Our bodies and hearts:
               Perpetual motion.

54

I am small
  Again
  Rounded to the bone
  Like a stone
  Washed over
   By salt
      Licking the edges
    Tossed and pulled
    By the larger force:
Wave energy breaking
        Me
  Free and wounding
My imagined wholeness:
Connection to the clump
In one cosmic
        Breath.

55

The heart
   It ceases to be free
An awkward pause
An abbreviated silence
   Into the foray of passion.
As a child would
   It lies in
  Hopes of getting
  A cookie,
     Fresh baked—
As if honesty
  Wouldn't do.

56

It's whole again
    Rising and arcing
  Steady and silent
     Ancient, wise
   Young and laughing
      Flirting
    With the earth
   As the full rays
     Illuminate
   Dance with me
     It calls.
     I twirl
      The trees sway,
     Blades hum,
      And the owl watches.
We make love.

57

It's happening again
The moon
Full and flat
Pasted against a wide-open
Yawn of a sky
Stillness steadying its gaze
Unto me
Blessing and bowing
Cradling and rocking
Adoring
Another discrete moment
Bridging the gap.

58

Tonight reminds me
It happened only once.
There are no
Endpoints—
A yawn,
A stretch
A wide-open moment:
Eternal.

59

The moon is full
   It stands between us
   As a magnet pulling
     Us towards
     The center of the orbit:
       Stillness in the core.
I stand here
  Reflections in the snow
My feet grow roots stretching
  Down
It's been so long
   In this field under its gaze.
Do you stand there
   Talking to the moon
   Instead
     Wanting me?
I feel us united
    In one place
     One time
      One thought
       One location:
        Full moon.

60

Longing
Bed after a long day
Work in the fields
    Hoeing, weeding, and sifting.

Hammock and lemonade
    Shading
  The heat of the day
Under arching arms
Of support
Our feet tangled at the edge.

That first jump
A leap of faith
Into cold, cold, cold
  Water,
Deep, translucent, free
Rebirthing
On such a hot languid day
Racing with you to the middle
    Childhood laughter
      A tender adult embrace
      A heavenly longing.

A warm fire
After a long snow sled
    Abandon and joy
      Stilling and melting
        Arm wrapped along my breast,
          Blood coursing through the veins
           Mittens by the stove
  As we thaw and melt
  Steady and still
An eternal stretch
As I tuck
The snowy hair behind your ear

      Dripping with your love
      Of the moment.

Christmas morning anticipation
      Of a child
Staring at you all wrapped
You are purple-lavender
With yellow jasmine cording.

I am red, alive
Dancing and jumping
A silver bow on my heart.

As a child
Time goes by
So slowly, but there is trust
And faith.

I wait for you by this
Fire to
Unwrap and bare
Our naked selves
With courage, faith,
And joy.

61

It's opaque
    Trust tells me
    It's there,
The clarity
    Of yesterday
    Is gone.

Today an obscuration,
    The shape
    Is evident,
But the detail is veiled.

    A full moon
        None
        The less.

62

I walk the hall
   And wonder
What it will feel like
To have your bare feet
    Against these worn boards.
How will you feel
    Walking down that hall
     Towards me
       To sleep?

63

I wish
  You were here
    To hold me
      Now.

64

Why aren't you
    In my
  Address book?

You've been in me
Pulsing to a beat
    In that moment
  Of heart.

You didn't wander
Or focus
Onto the thought:
Would I really love you?

Or even like you
Knew the depths
And read into my eyes
With a simple sigh.

65

My bed
      Reminds me of an amputee.
Once vibrant, stretching,
      Climbing and swinging
          On a spring day
              As an 8-year-old
        Or even a 34-year-old in the running
          Back and forth
      Now that side
        The right side
          Or left
            Depending on if you're in or out
      Is tucked still
          Made.
      My legs swing into that space
          At night
        As I cocoon into a fetal
          Position.
        It's all so still,
          Clean, neatly cut off, folded under, a hospital corner.
        Spring light hitting spring sheets.

It's Gone.
Like a Mack truck swerving off
    From the median
     Clipping me
    Below the belt.
    It's here, it's gone.
      It's severed.
    The nerves are still healing
      Dangling today
   As I hop about
    Without the appendage
   In a bed, in a house
   I am at peace in my heart.
    My mind in disbelief

    Sees that leg and knows
        It was once attached.
    It should be shocking.

The bed itself
    Is refreshing
Holding a place:
    Hope.
But it's like I forgot
    It was once alive and dancing.
    A younger age
        As an amputee.
    Now I am wholly myself.

GRIEF

G ood God
R age
I sle
E dgy
F rank

67

I am done
  Scouring the
    Ocean floor
For your words
    Walled and clasping
   Neon frequencies
  In the dark
   Unseen places.

Like a whale diving
  To and fro
Through the depths
  And ranges of
    These
   Wavelengths
I wait with sonar in
  Hand to locate you
Among your pod.

I've weathered countless
   Storms
Raging against the bow
Of this ship,
Days so long and
Short in light,
In order to
   GPS your location,
      Your move—
 As if only then
Could I steer my
  Vessel and boat.

You brought me
  Like a magnetic pull
Through the ages
  And continents

As you migrate
  To your feeding grounds,
Rich in nutrients and
The amber glow
As you spawn.

And then you pulled me
Down with such
Force as you
Descend like a
Bottom feeder.

68

The full circle
   Is knowing
  It's always in me.
She held that from me.
   You gave that to me
The gift,
   Like a ring on my finger
A wedding band to my beloved
   Self,
Is being able to love you
   Or anyone
And say, "No."

   Yet, always,
  The continuity flows
    Freely
    Like breathing in and out.
I am separate
   From the womb, the cord
     To the other.
   Finally, I have healed
   And, oh, my,
   Birthed
   Myself
To wholly connect
With one or another
 Me or you
 Heaven or earth
 Within or without—
 No and love can go
 Hand in hand.

My exhale is your inhale
Across
Oceans and depths
Lifetimes and ages

Your exhale
Is my inhale.
Always. Simply.
Although we may always
Be divided
By the oceans
As we settle into
Different continents
And passages
As we migrate
Through time and space
Never touching never
Ever loving ever.
Separate and delineated by
Choices and the word "no."

69

The full circle
Scrawls across my chest
Like some emblem,
A badge to patience,
Lessons learned,
Scars and wounding
Healed.
It's pinned there neatly,
Like a grandmother in her Sunday best
Or Saturday,
If she is Jewish.
A simple pin,
A gold circle,
Sits in my jewelry box.
I never liked it.
I inherited it.
Almost as if you knew
The course
I was on—
That one day
You would extend a hand across
Heavens and time
And be that grandmother again
Here and now
Saluting me saying
"Honey child, I love you."
Walking in Coolidge Corner,
Pumping my hand with each step
I am obviously your granddaughter,
Pride and love,
Stretch from your heart to mine,
One full circle, undivided.

But my heart like his
Was cold and shut you out
Because of her or him
Or really with a sigh

Just the confusion.
Nonetheless, this offering now to me on my 38th—
A full circle:
Womanly and swaying
Melting hearts and screaming love,
Dancing with genius and your pride—even
If I wasn't him.

You knew there was a time,
When you were gone
When the transect would be
Complete.
Whole.
I still feel the pain, the projection in my belly,
That I wasn't good enough.
Was that make-believe, a fairy tale?

More confusion, but I am still full and whole.
Wearing the clarity that you never could claim because you were
Bound to him. Jewish mothers and their sons
And their son's son
Eclipsed me like a
Bolt of lightning being pulled back
To darkness and the sky
In an instant.
Yet, you adored me, didn't you?

God, it's all so confused, the development is tainted
Like a spool of film
Exposed before it's fixed and adjusted
To light.
I have walked the path
That you did, too.
Haven't I?
Who are you? God, really, who are you?

70

Arrogance aside
I know now
That I am brilliant
I cannot squirm away under its grip
For it's me.

What's really funny
If we were doing comedy
Instead of tragedy
Is that she quite literally
Excavated and mummified
That radiance from me.
Squashed it
Like an angry heel
Digging into a half-dead mouse
And killing it, of course,
To spare it from further pain.
I think you earned another badge
That way. So thoughtful taking it and me
Out of my misery.
Then they all thought you were the queen
And I was the dunce in the dungeon.
Really so good of you to care for me,
Another badge.
If you were in the Girl Scouts—what?
You would be the envy of the pack.

Here I was locked in the basement, mute,
Some medieval torture thing going on,
Enacting history for the academic, of course.
Now you have my words and my light.

But I was so magnificent
That I just waited till
You looked the other way
And walked right past the drunken key master and never looked back.

71

The truth
For me lies
In these pages
Like rumpled sheets
Pressed in by a hangover
Or hangovers for the fun
And for me, the serious.

I could write:
And the queen smiled daily upon her servants
Filling them with just enough
To replenish
From this endeavor.
They gave great thanks
Again and again.
Amen.

She would think it was real.
That's the joke.
Or I could celebrate this newfound adult, separate and alive,
And speak the truth,
As I always do
Not for me, but for the volumes
Of unspoken ones—
The ones still
Gagged and in fear.

I am already flinching, the PTSD is flaring,
In anticipation of her personalizing
The whole damn journey.
I need to let them know I was scared too and I speak too
And I am separate too and I am safe too.

Quenching herself from me every damn sip
I am parched and she gets to the last drop
And doesn't even know the taste
Or sound of likeness

Or me.
She thinks she knows me.
I think
If I was vanilla, I am not
Even pure but just the imitation.

It's worse, much worse.
I am the sour taste in the fridge
That curls her lip
And puckers her rage
And lifts her fist
As if she were 6'5".
My bones thank their lucky stars
She's not
Armed.

An abuser teaches the abused
To swallow all the bad tastes
To become all the projections
To fight back just hard enough
When you are ten, eleven, fifteen, thirty-five,
To get slapped across the face
Every day until
You know
You bring the drink and dance around the room
Like a jester at 5:00 p.m.
You never do anything without asking
And you never get respect, you just give it away
Until your self-esteem is so low or
You are bruised and beaten
Just like she was
But can't ever know
Or ever share.

72

I need to shut down this joint, buster
I need to close this chapter, honey,

The drapes are pulled.
They are red and velvet, of course,
Just like the first ballet my mother took me to
When I was 6,
Christmas, *The Nutcracker*, of course,
Maybe 5, but I was so confused
In this fantasy
Because
My life was spinning and dancing
Ever so fast
I was always already
In my own little wonderland.

It wasn't until I was about 35
Until I figured out
How to get the storyline.
I watched mesmerized and my heart
Danced and jingled
Like the tree in that Jimmy Stewart movie,
That I have actually never seen fully,
But the jingle brought back my love for myself, and what an
Amazing child I was.

She may disagree depending on her mood
And how many times I have heard the ice clink against her glass
I can smell it from one end of the house to the other.
I miss walking through.
I miss the creaking floorboards and
The weathered molding
Timeless architecture:
Me, her, us—even the dog.
    A collective history.

So, I have pulled the curtain and am so hopeful for the next Stage. It's all a mystery.

73

It's like I am on the merry-go-round
I've made a full circle
On every animal
Hands wrapped
Around zebra neck
At 5
Going up and down
Ponies brown and black
White at 7
Rearing its legs
Like a stallion
I imagine.

And with deep gratitude

Other poetry titles by Wendy E. Slater:

Into the Hearth, Poems-Volume 14

Of the Flame, Poems-Volume 15

The Ocher of Abundance, Poems-Volume 16

The Perspective of Constellation, Poems-Volume 17

Visit Wendy E. Slater's website
www.traduka.com